Just
Imagine

Catherine Athans, Ph.D.

ANGELS ISLAND PRESS
Los Altos, CA

Angels Island Press
An Angels Island Production
303 First Street
Los Altos, CA 94022
www.AngelsIsland.com
1-888-58ANGEL

ISBN 978-0-9794380-1-2

Printed in the United States of America

DESIGN: DOTTI ALBERTINE, WWW.ALBERTINEBOOKDESIGN.COM
IMAGES: JUPITER IMAGES

Dedicated to all
who are courageous enough
to let their imaginations
run wild!

Just Imagine

Did you ever catch yourself drifting off in thought?

Did you ever wonder where you go?

Do you allow your mind free reign and allow yourself the fun of fantastic pictures, marvelous journeys, marvelous feelings?

Imagining stimulates the brain and creates wonderful hormones that make you happy.

Imagining allows your heart to be in coherence. It brings a sense of peace.

Catherine Athans, Ph.D.

Imagining provides you with a richer participation in your own life; for it is your imagination, your thoughts which create your perceptions of the world in which you live.

Please consider:
Nothing exists today that wasn't first Imagined!

Imagination is more than a faculty of the mind …
Imagination is a flowing, intuitive gift.

Imagination is the ability to see what could be.
Imagination is the bringing into being—
 from little or nothing—Great Richness …

Just Imagine

To invent,
to dream,
to create,
and to design
require first
the activation
of your
imagination.

*Allow your heart feelings, inklings
and ideas to take shape and form.*

Just Imagine

Please know that
your rich imagination
is the beginning
of your amazing
transformation!

It was in the active
imagination of your childhood
that your life's dreams, wishes,
and desires were first born.

Catherine Athans, Ph.D.

See how they grow.

…the vivid wonders
of childhood imagination
can still be yours …
Just allow them to be!

Feel yourself feeling Great …
Self-esteem is growing by the second.

Just Imagine

Did you know that it is in activating and using your imagination that you—your life force, your core, your very essence—become LARGER than when you dwelt in the world of rules and logic?

Allow yourself to dream of more.

Allow yourself to
Dream **BIG.**

YOU ARE ALIVE!

Having an active imagination is the first step to having the life you desire.

Your imagination is like a genie in a bottle

that has been corked up for years.

It's time to uncork the bottle

and see just what will happen!

And unlike the traditional genie who only offers three wishes, the wishes, dreams, and desires revealed through your imagination are

… boundless
… and limitless

Just Imagine

Please remember a time when you were
acknowledged for your vibrant imagination.

How did you feel?

Now allow yourself to have that feeling in the
present.

How do you feel now?

Catherine Athans, Ph.D.

Go back to a time when Mom, Dad, Grandma, Aunt,
Uncle or other adults thought you were the *cutest*
and the *best* when you were acting out a desire of
your heart.

Picture the love that was
in their eyes and on their faces.

GIVE THAT UNCONDITIONAL LOVE TO YOURSELF.

Just Imagine

What Imagination Can Accomplish

You may know the story of Olympic Gold medalist, Jim Thorpe: He practiced his broad jumps by lying in a hammock closing his eyes and visualizing the distance that he wanted to jump, and then visualized himself in every frame, every motion of the jump until he saw himself completing each jump.

As Jim lay in his hammock day after day, his coach became concerned and began to voice his concerns rather loudly. Jim's coach wanted to see Jim practicing and working out. One day, as Jim lay in his hammock with his eyes closed, Jim's coach came over to talk to him. Jim opened his eyes and told his coach he was glad to see him and asked the coach if he would be so kind as to step back another ten feet from the hammock.

Jim's coach was delighted to comply as he thought Jim was going to leap out of the hammock and finally get to work. Instead, Jim looked at the coach, then closed his eyes and gently resumed his gentle swing in the hammock.

The coach became upset and yelled, "Jim, when are you going to start practicing?"

 Jim opened one eye and responded,
"Coach, I already am."

Just Imagine

What Jim knew was that by using his imagination,
through focused visualization, he WAS *practicing*.

When you become willing
to use your imagination and all your senses,
and become willing to
DREAM A LARGE DREAM,
you begin to manifest your True desires.

This will lead you to attain what you desire,
which brings you to your Highest Good.

Unlimited choices exist in your imagination . . .

Check it out!

Take a moment here to stop and think about your choices. Jot these down in your journal.

*How did you come to make the choices
you made about life in general? Career? Family?*

*Were your choices governed by logic, reason, or fear?
Was your intuition or heart's desire involved?*

*Please consider that your Heart holds the keys
to unlock the doors to your great . . .
HAPPINESS, SATISFACTION, and JOY.*

Just Imagine

It is in using your imagination that channels of joy and delight are created. Think about this a few moments.

It is in using your imagination
That channels of joy and delight are created.

One of the reasons I wrote this book is to help you understand the importance of having an active imagination …

Allow your imagination to bring you back to TRUTH.

Using your imagination is vital to your *very* existence, for it is in using your imagination that you achieve levels of *inspiration* previously unknown.

Inspiration literally means to INFUSE WITH LIFE.

**Through using your imagination
you literally make more room for "life" in you.**

As you practice activating your imagination, your perception of the physical world will broaden. The limits that time and life may have placed upon your imagination will begin to fall away . . .

You will find that all your senses and your ability to *vision and imagine* will become much more robust.

Just Imagine

*It is from this newly robust and active imagination
that abundance will be created.*

In using your imagination, you will achieve a
personal reality that is RICH, LUSH, FULFILLING,
and SATISFYING.

You will enrich your life, rediscovering your creativity,
and finding a new **ZEST FOR LIFE.**

An active imagination is also key

to exploring and developing new opportunities

and possibilities in all areas of your life.

The Lock Is Rusty

Perhaps you are now thinking, "Catherine, my lock is rusty, my keys don't seem to work. When I try to go into my imagination I become distracted by the thoughts of what I should be doing such as mowing the lawn or doing the dishes, or I start thinking about what happened at work."

Perhaps for some of you, when you first go to use your imagination, you find you come up blank.

How do you get past this?

A simple way is to begin by thinking of your favorite television character or your favorite character from a book. Choose someone who has qualities that you admire and would want to have as your own.

Now *imagine* that character as yourself. Go first for the general picture. Picture yourself wearing the same or similar clothes as your chosen character.

Note the shoes and accessories that you are wearing. Continue to fill in your mind's picture.

Put yourself in a particular setting.
Are you outside or inside?
Are there people around you or are you alone?

Just Imagine

Think about what you would want to eat when choosing a meal. Think about how, as this character, you would interact with others. This is when the magic begins to happen …

Now, imagine yourself TODAY, in rich detail, doing those things that you would want to draw into your life. Then do what you can TODAY to take you a step closer to these changes.

Your action works as a prayer or statement which comes to affirm these attributes as part of you.

Even if at first it doesn't seem real,
ACT AS IF IT IS.

Act as You Wish to Be

Socrates stated, *"Act as you wish to be."* To act is to bring it into being, and the first step to *acting as you wish to be* is activating your imagination. For so many of us, we lament the position in which we find ourselves. We wish someone else to move us. We *negate* the power within that is the *only* real guide that will tell us the *truth* for our life.

Just Imagine

So let go the outside; practice coming inside.

Let your imagination run wild.

Be an adventurer of your own soul.

Be willing to see what you really are.

What we continuously imagine clearly,

is impressed upon the subconscious mind,

and carried out in the minutest detail.

Allow your imagination to carry out

your heart's wishes, dreams, and desires.

Imagination as a Precious Gift

You may use your imagination to alter your mood, your response to what is going on around you, your daily interactions, your inner feelings, and physical manifestations which flow from above.

Think of your imagination as a precious gift,

for an imagination can have

a profound effect on both your mind and body.

An active imagination has such a force in and on your life it can be used for much broader healing.

Just Imagine

Research has shown that activating a person's imagination assists in the healing and treatment of various physical, mental, and emotional illnesses—including heart disease, hypertension, post-traumatic stress disorder, and arterial sclerosis.

As Florence Scovell Shin shares, *"What man images, sooner or later, externalizes in his affairs."*

She goes on further to explain, "I know of a man who feared a certain disease. It was a very rare disease and difficult to get, but he pictured it continually and read about it until it manifested in his body, and he died, the victim of *distorted imagination*."

Use Your Imagination to Heal

The Simingtons of Texas (husband and wife physician team) developed a creative visualization process for terminal cancer patients to use to fight and prevail against that dreaded disease.

An activated imagination
can reduce stress and help with healing.

An activated imagination can also
create openings and shift energy
which result in visible, measurable changes.

Just Imagine

Through your focused

thoughts and intentions,

YOU CAN ALTER MATTER.

Just Imagine

Take a Different Path

Right now you have the ability, through your imagination, to choose how you will respond. For example, perhaps you and your employer interact in ways that leave you feeling stressed.

Or perhaps certain exchanges between you and a friend, your partner, your child, or your parent leave you feeling powerless, weak or dissatisfied. You want to experience encounters which result in different outcomes.

Catherine Athans, Ph.D.

Use your imagination
to paint a different picture,
to write a different script,
to change your position,
to transmute your feelings.

Through your imagination, picture in your mind what it is that you want in your life.

Allow the ideal situation to form pictures in your mind and place your self in those pictures.

Just Imagine

Give them texture and color.

This is the starting point for change.

It may take a little time for the changes to occur, but don't lose heart.

THE CHANGES WILL OCCUR!

Please know that the changes are now occurring even if they are not currently visible to you.

Let's apply this to an actual situation in your life:
Take a moment now and explore a few ways that
you can immediately effect change by using your
imagination.

DEVELOP A VISION of yourself acting in a way that
you want to act in your next encounter with your
boss or a family member.

Next, use your physical senses as a starting point
toward building a stronger imagination.
ENVISION what you are wearing, see yourself sitting
at your desk or at a table.

Just Imagine

What you would like to have happen in this encounter? **BE SPECIFIC** and **FOCUSED**.
What would bring you joy, happiness, or peace?

Now, reinforce your imaginative thoughts by taking physical action:

WRITE down the words you are using in this encounter with your boss or family member while you are calm, cool, collected and intelligent.

Now develop a vision of how you are going to feel in your next interaction with this other person. Focus.

FEEL what it's like to have your emotions in a place that *you* have chosen.

TRUST that what you are imagining from your heart is being created as you are imagining it.

Make time to go inside and experience what it is you are truly feeling, for from every interaction, you have an opportunity for growth.

Breathe.

Relax.

Give yourself permission to acknowledge stuck energy and then activate your imagination to get unstuck.

Just Imagine

START FROM WHERE YOU ARE and apply this imagination to your inner feelings and transmute them into something positive by changing your attitude and viewing additional possibilities.

Now, release negative feelings and experience a lightness of thought and body. Let go and feel the new possibilities.

Go back into the above encounter and use your sight, hearing, touch, taste, and smell to provide richer details.

Understand that by this very exercise you have already created change!

Through the use of your imagination, you have shifted your energy. This shift will have an immediate and substantial effect in how you respond to your employer or family member.

Remember…
It is through the use of your imagination
that you can open space or close space.

You can bring forth

And you can let go.

Just Imagine

It is through using your imagination
that you make manifest or make dissolve.

*Think **BIG***

If your first thoughts are large, lush, but then you
start to think, "Oh, no, this is too big. I need to ask for
less." Please immediately stop yourself!

Please continue to affirm the larger desire
THE BIGGEST ONE YOU CAN IMAGINE!

Allowing yourself to be childlike and imagining
in great abundance will actually speed along the
manifestation of what you are imagining because
you are letting go of judgment.

Take Steps:

If it is more comfortable for you, you may first choose to imagine obtaining your heart's desire through a series of smaller steps, like the steps up to your dream home.

Know that if your heart is in harmony with your soul, things happen immediately.
They are not labor intensive. The actions you carry out follow the inner guidance you receive, the hunches you get.

Just Imagine

As the universe is infinite,

so too is your imagination.

What you want is already there.

Allow it to occur in your life at this time.
Say to yourself:

This or something greater, God.

BE GRATEFUL FOR WHERE YOU ARE NOW.
Don't limit your self.

When you make it *smaller,* you *limit* your *SELF,* and you put limits on God, because limitation is not the Divine Mind's plan for you.

This limiting is your three-dimensional mind, not your Divine Mind.

"Imagination is far more important than knowledge."
—ALBERT EINSTEIN

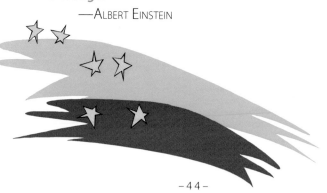

 *Just Imagine*

Imagination Energizes Intuition

Intuition is something that many people have been conditioned to ignore. Intuitive impulses, hunches, and gut feelings too often take a back seat to pure logic.

The imagination is a flowing, intuitive organism.

Whenever you have a hunch,
take a moment to jot it down.

 Write out your hunch in as much detail and description as you can.

Use adjectives and adverbs to expand the picture. Be sure to include aromas, fragrances, sounds, colors, and movement.

Keep a record of all your strong hunches so that you can go back and study them at your leisure.

Scientific studies show

that there is an intimate relationship

between the mind and the body.

You imagine with BOTH the body and the mind.
 Physical activity can bring inspiration, and your five senses can bring you into a highly receptive mental state.

Just Imagine

Imagination can bring real, physical results. By following through on your dreams, you can create the world that you want to be in.

It is your imagination which first brings to consciousness the facts of your inner being.

Imagination is Powerful.

When you have imagined what it is that you
would like manifested in your life, please send your
thoughts and pictures off with the following words:

Under grace, in a perfect way,
I release you to be wonderfully created
and I open my arms wide to allow you
into my life with ease and joy.

Just Imagine

By using these words, you are freeing all thought forms and allowing the Source to create. Please know that these words are vital.

By freeing the thought forms, you have made a space to receive even more of what you desire.

An Active Imagination

provides a Myriad of Potential Paths

for Your Life.

Catherine Athans, Ph.D.

One of the greatest uses of your time is time spent using the gift of imagination. Imagination expands your possibilities and your mind beyond the logical and scientific into a realm where your dreams can come true.

Know that the body and the mind

should be equal and balanced

for mental, physical, and spiritual health.

Please become a more engaged participant in your life through encouraging your imagination to be **FERTILE, ACTIVE**, and **BOUNDLESS.**

Just Imagine

**Realize that the use of your imagination
—the way that you think and perceive—
creates the reality that you experience.**

Use your imagination to follow through on your
dreams to create the kind of life activities which are

loving,

joyful,

interesting,

and

satisfying to you.

Catherine Athans, Ph.D.

Activating Your Imagination Activities

Activating Your Imagination can be both fun and exciting. Allow your mind and emotions to roam free. See open doors instead of blank walls. Employing all your senses, visualize in rich colors, varying textures, and a myriad of scents.

For a few of you, unleashing your imagination may at first be a little scary as perhaps you haven't allowed yourself to use your imagination in some time.

Just Imagine

To start, imagine that you have just bitten into a very sour pickle. What happened in your mouth?

Your thoughts and imagination brought about a *physical response*. While the pickle imagery was simple, science has proven that imagination can alter your very cell structure. I ask that as you work through these exercises and start re-activating your imagination, you permit yourself to use your imagination to put thoughts and ideas together that may not as yet make sense.

Give Your Imagination Free Reign

1. Using your imagination, think of a warm, rich, loving place, full of colors, tones, vibrations, smells, feelings, and textures. Please write a paragraph on what you are now feeling in your heart. Please write a paragraph on what you are feeling in your belly. Are they the same? What are the differences, if any?

2. Using your imagination, think of an inner quality that you have admired in someone. Imagine yourself with that quality. Please write a paragraph on how having that quality would affect your life. Write it in the present tense: *I have this wonderful quality of …*

Please write a paragraph on how having that quality would affect the lives of those you care for.

3. Using your imagination, think about spring. Act as if it is now next spring. Imagine nature in bloom and a time of rebirth. Using your imagination, write down where and what you will be doing next spring. Remember to put action in your picture.

4. Using your physical senses assists you in awakening the consciousness of your imagination. The next time you have a chance, pick up a piece of fruit. Use your senses. Look at the fruit. Touch the skin of the fruit. Is it soft? Is it hard?

Is it smooth or is it rough? Now smell it. Is it sweet or bitter? Does is smell tangy? Now open the fruit. What do you see? Does it smell different? Does it feel different? What is the sound when it was opened? Did it sound crisp? Did it squelch? Did it sound juicy? Now taste it with your eyes closed. Now taste it with your eyes opened. Is there a difference? If so, what?

5. There exists a connection between words and thought. Write your first thoughts to the following words or phrases:

Just Imagine

- *Joy . . .*
- *Greatness . . .*
- *Red Velvet . . .*
- *Lushness . . .*
- *Morning Tide . . .*
- *Abundance . . .*

6. Imagine yourself being able to fly. Where would you go? How would things looks from the air? Would you land and look around? Write a story about this. Make it in the present tense.

7. Imagine yourself having a day that you consider to be perfect. How does your day go? Who do you spend time with? Where are you? Remember the sky is endless and so is your imagination. Embellish it. Make it BIG. Make it in the NOW.

8. Imagine yourself on a wonderful vacation. Is it warm or cold? Are you alone? Is it peaceful or noisy? Do you find that you are limiting yourself to only those things which are practical or possible?

FINAL THOUGHTS

Be truthful with yourself at all times.

Allow your imagination to develop.

Give yourself the time you need.

Be grateful and give praise for what is in your life now and what is being drawn to you.

Have fun!

Allow yourself to be childlike.

Explore.

Be silly.

Experience more richness in your life.

Also by Catherine Athans, Ph.D.

Make Your Dreams Come True Now!

Who Do You Think You Are Anyway?
(August 2010)